FOCUS

OCEANS
AND SEAS

KINGFISHER

First published 2017 by Kingfisher
an imprint of Macmillan Children's Books
20 New Wharf Road, London N1 9RR
Associated companies throughout the world
www.panmacmillan.com

Series editor: Hayley Down
Design: Jeni Child

ISBN 978-0-7534-4106-0

9 8 7 6 5 4 3 2 1

1TR/0417/WKT/UG/128MA

A CIP catalogue record for this book is available from the British Library.

Printed in China

Picture credits
The Publisher would like to thank the following for permission to reproduce their material.
Top = t; Bottom = b; Middle = m; Left = l; Right = r
Front cover: Getty/Westend61 - Gerald Nowak; Back cover: Shutterstock; Cover flap: Shutterstock/Krzysztof Odziomek; Page 1 iStock/LFPuntel; 3 iStock/allianoi;
4–5 iStock/Arnar; 4t iStock/cinoby; 4b iStock/yangwenshuang; 5m iStock/tiverylucky; 6–7 iStock/xingmin07; 8–9 iStock/shalamov; 10t iStock/ paulprescott72;
10m iStock/VargaJones; 10b iStock/Jewelsy; 11t (b/g) iStock/7maru; 11t Getty/Inaki Relanzon; 11m Shutterstock/BlueOrange Studio; 11b Shutterstock/Bernhard
Staehli; 12–13 Getty/Chris & Monique Fallows; 14–15 iStock/akrp; 15 Shutterstock/Mykola Mazuryk; 16 (1) Getty/Werner Van Steen; 17tl (2) iStock/SeppFriedhuber;
17tl (3) Alamy/Chris Howarth/ South Atlantic; 17m (4) iStock/Justinreznick; 17 (5) iStock/shauni; 17bl (6) iStock/Ssviluppo; 17tr (7) SeaPics; 17tr (8) Alamy/
Manfred Gottschalk; 17mr (9) Getty/Toshi Sasaki; 17br (10) Creative Commons; 18–19 Shutterstock/Perfect Lazybones; 18t Shutterstock/IM_photo; 18m iStock/
ShaunWilkinson; 18b Shutterstock/Patryk Kosmider; 19t iStock/cinoby; 19m iStock/ultramarinfoto; 19b Shutterstock/Dmyttro Pylypenko; 20 Getty/Chris Cheadle;
21t iStock/aiisha5; 21m iStock/SeppFriedhuber; 21b Shutterstock/Anibal Trejo; 22–23 Alamy/Nature Picture Library; 24–25 iStock/cdwheatley; 24t iStock/KGrif;
24b iStock/DeeAnn-Cranston; 25t Getty/wildestanimal; 25b Alamy/Miden Pictures; 26 Shutterstock/betsazar; 27t Alamy/Karen Black; 27m Shutterstock/KYTan;
27b iStock/rocketegg; 28–29 iStock/Alex-Lindbloom; 30 iStock/ericsphotography; 31t Shutterstock; 31b Alamy/Nature Picture Library; 32t iStock/flyingdouglas;
32bl iStock/michakloowijk; 32br iStock/Trevorplatt; 33tl iStock/Harry-Eggens; 33tr iStock/pchoui; 33bl iStock/ChristianWilkinson; 33br iStock/BirdImages; 34
(1) Alamy/WaterFrame; 35tl (2) Alamy/National Geographic Creative; 35tl (3) Getty/Alexander Semenov; 35m (4) Shutterstock/Krzysztof Odziomek; 35bl (5)
Alamy/Justin Hofman; 35bl (6) Alamy/WaterFrame; 35tr (7) iStock/aschaffer; 35tr (8) Alamy/AF Archive; 35m (9) SeaPics/Hideyuki Utsunomiya; 35br (10)
Alamy/Niels Poulsen; 36 Alamy/RGB Ventures/SuperStock; 37t Alamy/Nature Picture Library; 37m Alamy/Nature Picture Library; 37b iStock/webguzs; 38 iStock/
KenCanning; 39t Alamy/blickwinkel; 39b Alamy/ imageBROKER; 40 (1) Getty/Chris&Monique Fallows; 41tl (2) iStock/Subaquesshutterbug; 41tl (3) iStock/Malbert;
41m (4) iStock/vicnt; 41bl (5) iStock/EXTREME-PHOTOGRAPHER; 41bl (6) iStock/yangwenshuang; 41 tr (7) iStock/berndneeser; 41tr iStock/singularone; 41m (9)
Shutterstock/Laura Dinraths; 41br (10) iStock/ShaneGross; 42–43 Alamy/WaterFrame; 44–45 Getty/Gerard Soury; 45 Alamy/Design Pics Inc; 46 iStock/vojce;
47t iStockShubhashish5; 47m FLPA/Karl Van Ginderdeuren; 47b Alamy/SolvinZankl; 48 (1) FLPA/Norbert Wu; 49tl (2) FLPA/Photo Researchers; 49tl (3) iStock/
LindaZ; 49m (4) Alamy/Minden Pictures; 49bl (5) Alamy/Kelvin Aitken; 49bl (6) Getty/PETER SCOONES; 49TR (7) FLPA/Photo Researchers; 49tl (8) FLPA/Photo
Researchers 49m (9) Alamy/NOAA; 49br (10) Getty/UMI NO KAZE; 50–51 iStock/Lukasz Szczepanski; 52 iStock/Bob Balestri; 53t iStock/VuCongDanh; 54–55
Getty/Paul Nicklen; 56t iStock/tiverylucky; 56bl iStock/RainervonBrandis; 56br Shutterstok/Rich Carey; 57t iStock/iShootPhotosLLC; 57bl iStock/maxoidos; 57br
iStock/tacojim; 58 (1) iStock/betoon; 59tl (2) iStock/EpicStockMedia; 59tl (3)iStock/amriphoto; 59m (4) iStock/ChuckSchugPhotography; 59bl (5)iStock/JMichl;
59bl (6) iStock/technotr; 59tr (7) iStock/rainerhi; 59tr (8) iStock/Alan_Lagadu; 59m (9) Getty/Paul Kennedy; 59br (10) iStock/danulis; 61 iStock/skynesher; 62
iStock/strmko; 63 iStock/Yann-HUBERT; 64 iStock/crisho.

IN FOCUS

OCEANS AND SEAS

BY STEVE PARKER

KINGFISHER

CONTENTS

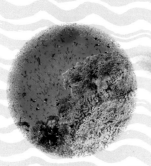

WATER WORLD

Arctic Ocean

Atlantic Ocean

Pacific Ocean

Atlantic Ocea

THE EARTH'S SURFACE

FAST FACT

is covered by ...

Seas and oceans:
352 million sq km

Rivers and lakes:
9 million sq km

Land: 149 million sq km

Southern Ocean

Our planet is called "the Earth", but maybe it should be "the Ocean"! Over two-thirds of its surface is covered by the salty water of oceans and seas. That's twice as much as all the land and the fresh (non-salty) water of rivers and lakes. Seas and oceans are the biggest, deepest, strangest and most exciting places in the world. Let's explore them!

PERCENTAGE OF WATER ON THE EARTH:

Seas and oceans: 96.5

Ice caps, glaciers and snow: 1.7

Under the ground: 1.6

Lakes and rivers: less than 0.2

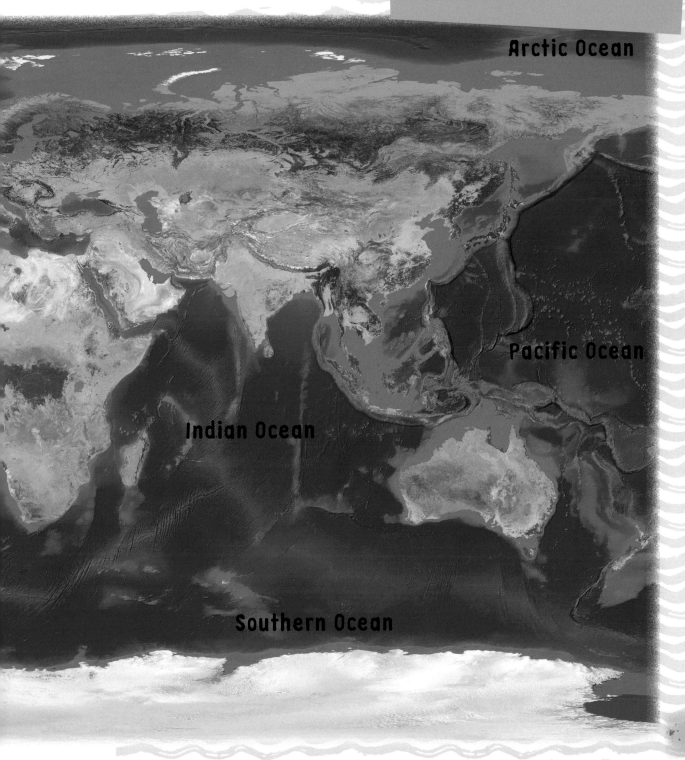

Arctic Ocean

Pacific Ocean

Indian Ocean

Southern Ocean

PLANET OCEAN

FAMOUS FIVE

The Earth may look like it has one giant ocean, but we have divided it into five parts – each with different features!

ARCTIC OCEAN

Area: 16 million square kilometres
% of the Earth's surface covered: 3
Average depth: 1205 m
Greatest depth: 5620 m

The Arctic is the smallest, shallowest and coldest ocean. In winter, it is mostly covered in floating sheets and lumps of ice. Even in summer there is floating ice in the middle, at the North Pole.

ATLANTIC OCEAN

Area: 85 million square kilometres
% of the Earth's surface covered: 17
Average depth: 3925 m
Greatest depth: 9220 m

The Atlantic has huge waves and fierce **hurricanes**. Much of its coastline is rocky with tall cliffs. It is divided into two almost equal parts: the North and South Atlantic Oceans.

INDIAN OCEAN

Area: 70 million square kilometres
% of the Earth's surface covered: 14
Average depth: 3960 m
Greatest depth: 7455 m

The Indian Ocean is the warmest, with many large and small islands, and beautiful coral reefs. It is usually calm, apart from monsoon storms that bring rain to South Asia from July to September.

PACIFIC OCEAN

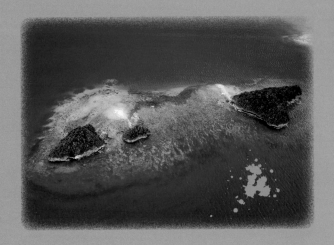

Area: 169 million square kilometres
% of the Earth's surface covered: 33
Average depth: 4030 m
Greatest depth: 11,033 m

The widest ocean, the Pacific covers almost one-third of the Earth. It has more than 20,000 islands. Some have no people and almost no animals – apart from a few seabirds!

SOUTHERN OCEAN

Area: 22 million square kilometres
% of the Earth's surface covered: 4
Average depth about: 4500 m
Greatest depth: 7235 m

Wild and stormy in winter, the Southern Ocean has the strongest average winds on the Earth. It has many huge icebergs that break free from the great ice-covered land mass of Antarctica.

GO WITH THE FLOW

Oceans and seas are never still. Even when the surface looks calm, water is moving beneath, as flowing currents. These vary from a small, gentle drift along the shore to gigantic torrents as millions of tonnes of water rush through the deep ocean faster than you can run!

Riding currents:

Animals that travel long distances swim with currents to help speed their journeys. Blue sharks cross the North Atlantic with the Gulf Stream to reach Europe, then head south to ride the North Equatorial Current back to North America.

WAVES AND TIDES

Your questions about waves answered, including what makes them!

What is a tsunami?

A tsunami is caused by an **earthquake** under the ocean. The shifting seabed makes a massive ripple of water that travels hundreds of kilometres. When it reaches land, it surges ashore as a giant wave, causing terrible damage.

How are waves made?

Far out in the ocean, wind heaps up large ridges of water called swells. As the swells move towards the shore, water piles up above the shallow seabed into tall waves that topple over, or break, and crash roaring white foam onto the land.

How do tides happen?

Tides are due to the **gravity**, or pull, of the Moon and the Sun. Gravity pulls the Earth's water nearest the Moon or Sun into a bulge, making a high tide! As the Earth spins each day, the bulges travel around it, about once every 12½ hours.

Why do some places have big tides, others almost none?

Where currents and tidal waters flow into a narrow area between land on either side, the tidal range (the difference between high and low tides) is greater. On straight, open coasts the range is smaller. Try pouring the same amount of water into a bowl and a drinking glass – the water will be higher in the glass, because there is less room to spread out.

TOP 10

OCEAN WONDERS

Far below the waves are some of the Earth's biggest, most spectacular sights – if you have a submarine!

Mid-Atlantic Ridge

At 16,000 kilometres long, this split in the middle of the Atlantic is the world's longest **mountain range**. This diver is exploring a **fissure** called the Silfra Crack.

North Pole

The North Pole is under drifting ice sheets in the Arctic Ocean. If you plant a flag on the ice above the North Pole, it will float away.

Monterey Canyon

This canyon is near California, USA. At 150 kilometres long, it is similar to the Grand Canyon and is home to strange deep-sea animals!

Tristan da Cunha

Far out in the South Atlantic, 2400 kilometres from mainland Africa, this tiny place is the Earth's most isolated island.

Cape Horn

Fierce storms blow at the tip of South America, where the Pacific and Atlantic Oceans meet. Winds there rage at over 100 kilometres per hour.

Mauna Kea

This Hawaiian peak is the tallest **seamount**. At 10,000 metres tall, it's even higher than Mount Everest!

Waterspouts

Florida Keys is a great place to spot these tall, twisting funnels of water-spray and drops. Similar to **tornadoes** on land, some reach over 1000 metres into the sky!

Bay of Fundy

The world's biggest tides are on Canada's east coast. The water flows into a narrow inlet, creating tides of over 16 metres!

Mariana Trench

In the Western Pacific is the deepest place on the Earth: 11 kilometres below sea level. Only two crewed vessels have been there, in 1960 (pictured) and 2012.

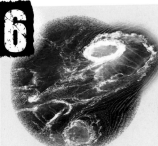

Maelstrom of Saltstraumen

Near Norway, currents and tides combine as whirlpools, called *maelstroms*, swirling at 50 kilometres per hour!

Which wonder would you like to explore?

SUPER SEAS!

A sea is a very large area of water that is partly surrounded by land, usually at the edge of an ocean. There are more than 100 seas on the Earth!

CARIBBEAN SEA

Area: 2.75 million sq km
Average depth: 2200 m
The Caribbean Sea is one of the warmest, with many coral reefs and a string of tropical islands to the north and the east.

NORTH SEA

Area: 0.57 million sq km
Average depth: 95 m
Very shallow and often stormy, the North Sea is busy with ships, oil rigs and enormous wind farms that produce clean energy!

MEDITERRANEAN SEA

Area: 2.5 million sq km
Average depth: 1500 m
The Mediterranean Sea is mostly warm and calm. Nicknamed the "Med", it has busy holiday centres around its beautiful beaches.

SOUTH CHINA SEA

Area: 3.5 million sq km
Average depth: 2600 m
Thousands of ships criss-cross this sea carrying goods or tourists between the islands.

RED SEA

Area: 0.44 million sq km
Average depth: 485 m
Teeming with tropical fish and other creatures, the Red Sea is very warm, rarely rough and is surrounded by deserts.

CORAL SEA

Area: 4.8 million sq km
Average depth: 2400 m
Usually sunny with sparkling waters, the Coral Sea can be whipped up by tropical cyclones. The Great Barrier Reef is found here.

WEDDELL SEA

Area: 2.8 million sq km
Average depth: 2300 m
Like a huge bay partly enclosed by Antarctica, the Weddell Sea is frozen over in winter and crowded with icebergs the rest of the year.

OCEAN EDGES

Ocean and land constantly battle each other! When a river erodes (wears away) its banks, **shingle**, sand and mud are made and washed into the sea, where flat areas of land known as **bars** and **spits** may form. When a volcano erupts and its hot, runny **lava** flows into the water, the lava can cool into a solid rock island. In other places, the ocean wins as great storms, crashing waves and powerful currents erode the land.

FAST FACT

Tall, dark **CLIFFS** are made of hard rock, usually granite or basalt. The waves wear away or undercut the base to leave an overhang, which eventually tumbles into the sea. White cliffs are usually made of chalk rock, which is soft.

overhang
cliff

mangroves

FAST FACT

In **TROPICAL AREAS** where tides, waves and currents are gentle, mud collects along the shore and mangrove trees can grow. Where currents and tides are stronger, long, sandy beaches form.

FAST FACT

CURRENTS, WINDS, WAVES and **TIDES** wear rocks or ice into amazing shapes, such as caves, arches and tall, upright columns called stacks. A big storm may tear them down in seconds.

iceberg

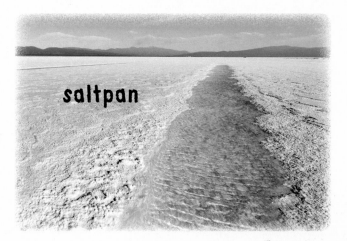

saltpan

FAST FACT

In flat, shallow areas, water can **EVAPORATE** (dry up) to reveal saltpans. These are areas of land covered by glistening sea salt, left behind by the water.

OCEAN LIFE

HOME SWEET HOME

Your questions about wonderful ocean habitats answered!

Which habitats are between land and sea?

Coastal habitats vary from smooth mudflats to steep cliffs. Along the **low tide mark** and in the **shallows** are many kinds of seaweeds. They are home to crabs, shellfish and animals that feed on them, such as sea otters!

Where does most ocean wildlife live?

Living things thrive in calm, shallow, sunlit waters – especially in the **tropics**! Some animals here have bright colours, but others blend in with their background; this is called **camouflage**. In some places, coral reefs grow.

What's the biggest habitat in the world?

The open ocean covers more than half of the Earth, and most of it is over 3000 metres deep. This is the realm of the world's biggest, fastest, fiercest predators, such as sharks, swordfish and orcas. It is also home to the world's most massive beasts: whales!

Where is it always dark and almost freezing?

Vast areas of the deep ocean bed are flat plains, covered with muddy ooze. There is no light or warmth from the sun, so it is dark and cold all the time. Strange fish, worms, prawns, crabs, sponges and starfish have adapted to this never-changing habitat.

ALONG THE SHORE

Shores are tough places to live! Plants and animals endure hot sun, drying winds, soaking rain, roaring waves, swishing currents and the constant rise and fall of the tide. Muddy and sandy shores may look empty when the tide is out, but many creatures are hiding beneath the surface.

As the tide rises, animals come out to search for food. Rocky coasts have big boulders and sheltered rockpools, teeming with fish and other animals. But the stones on shingle and pebble beaches are rolled around by the waves, making it hard for living things to survive on these shores.

FAST FACT

SEA TURTLES come to sandy beaches to lay their eggs. The female digs a pit with her flippers, lays eggs in the bottom, covers them with sand and then lumbers slowly back to the sea ...

turtle hatchling

... Months later, **TURTLE** hatchlings crack out of their egg and dig their way to the surface. They race to the sea as fast as possible to avoid being eaten by predators on the way.

anemone

They look like flowers, but **ANEMONES** are animals—and they're hungry! They catch prey, such as fish and shrimp, in their stinging tentacles and pass it into their mouth in the centre of their body.

FAST FACT

FAST FACT

The **COCONUT CRAB** is big and strong. It can live out of water for hours, or even days. It eats almost anything, from seeds and leaves to rotting plants or old meat. It also climbs trees!

coconut crab

mudskipper

FAST FACT

MUDSKIPPERS dig a burrow where they hide from enemies. They can jump and skip very fast using their front fins and tail, as they hunt for small worms, shellfish and other prey.

CLOSE UP

CORAL WONDERLAND

Coral reefs cover less than 1 per cent of all the oceans' area, yet they are home to 25 per cent of ocean animals. Reefs are made of small, simple animals, called coral polyps. Polyps build stony cases around themselves. As they die and more grow, the cases build up into the reef's beautiful shapes.

The Great Barrier Reef:

Off the coast of north-east Australia, the Great Barrier Reef is the Earth's biggest coral reef. It is almost 2300 kilometres long and from 50 to 250 kilometres wide. It is home to over 600 kinds of coral, 3000 different shellfish and 1600 types of fish!

SEA ANEMONES are named after the anemone flower on land because their tentacles look like petals.

CORAL REEFS

Find out the facts about the reef's most fascinating inhabitants!

The **CLOWNFISH** has a special, slimy body covering, which protects it against an anemone's stings. The fish keeps the anemone clean by eating scraps of its leftover food.

CLEANER SHRIMPS walk gently over larger fish and other animals to pick off old scales, skin pests and other small bits. This helps the bigger creature stay clean – and the shrimp gets a meal!

Long, sharp, stinging spines make some **STARFISH** dangerous reef-dwellers. The big crown-of-thorns starfish is especially venomous and damages reefs by eating coral polyps.

POWDER BLUE TANGS grow to 25 centimetres long. A sharp spine at the base of their tail protects them against enemies.

Lurking in a cave or crack, the **MORAY EEL** can dart its head out and bite in a flash.

The **GIANT GROUPER** is more than 2.5 metres long and weighs over 350 kilograms. It lies in wait among the coral and is so massive it can swallow a small turtle or baby shark in one gulp!

The **BLACKTIP REEF SHARK** grabs any prey it can, including fish, squid, crabs, seabirds and even young seals!

Up to 1 metre across, the **GIANT CLAM** weighs as much as three adult humans! It sucks in water to filter out bits of food, and closes its shell against enemies.

A **SEAHORSE** sucks food through its tube-like mouth. Its tail holds onto seaweed or coral.

Western gulls

SPECTACULAR

PELICAN

The brown pelican flaps slowly above the sea, spots a fish and dives at speed into the water. After grabbing the fish, it pushes most of the water out of its balloon-like throat pouch before gulping down the meal.

brown pelican

STORM PETREL

The storm petrel is tiny – hardly the size of a garden sparrow. Yet, apart from during **breeding** time, it spends almost every minute in the air. Its main food is small fish and similar creatures. It picks them from the water's surface as it swoops down or "patters" by running along the surface.

storm petrel

sea eagle

puffins

SEABIRDS

Oceans are a great source of food for seabirds. These birds can be as small as your hand or as long as an adult human!

ALBATROSS

The wandering albatross has the longest wings of any bird! Each wing is as long as an adult person is tall! This huge bird glides for hours without flapping, and stays airborne for a year or more. It skims low over the waves to grab small fish and squid.

albatross

GANNET

When it spies a fish below, the northern gannet folds back its wings and dives like a feathery arrow. It hits the water at 100 kilometres per hour – as fast as a car on the motorway! It flaps its strong webbed feet to chase prey that swims as deep as 20 metres below the water's surface.

gannet

TOP 10

OCEAN CHAMPIONS

There are lots of record-breaking ocean creatures, including the biggest, longest, fastest and most numerous – and don't forget the floppiest!

 ## Blue whale

The biggest creature ever to live on the Earth, the blue whale can be 30 metres long and weigh over 150 tonnes. It eats four tonnes of food every day!

2 Leatherback turtle

At 700 kilograms in weight and 4 metres across, this is the biggest turtle and eats almost nothing but jellyfish!

3 Lion's mane jellyfish

The bell (body) of the lion's mane reaches 2.5 metres across. Its stinging tentacles trail for 30 metres or more.

4 Whale shark

Weighing 20 tonnes, the biggest fish is the whale shark. It swims with its huge mouth open to catch krill!

5 Krill

Small cousins of shrimps and prawns, krill are among the world's most numerous creatures. They are the main food for fish, squid and even great whales!

6 Saltwater crocodile

Biggest of all reptiles, the aggressive "saltie" grows to 7 metres and weighs over 1 tonne.

7 Sailfish

Fastest in the sea, the sailfish folds its top fin along its back. At 110 kilometres per hour, it's almost as fast as a cheetah is on land!

8 Super squid

Huge jumbo squid, and even bigger giant and colossal squid, prowl the ocean. They are the largest invertebrates (animals without a backbone).

9 Oarfish

Like a sea serpent of stories and legends, the oarfish is the longest bony fish. It can stretch for 11 metres – more than the longest snake, the python.

10 Sunfish

This is the heaviest fish with a bony **skeleton**. Weighing over 2 tonnes, it reaches 4.5 metres in length, and the same in height.

Which record breaker is your number one?

FREEZING OCEANS

Salty seawater doesn't freeze until it reaches minus two degrees Celsius. Some animals can cope with the near-freezing polar waters – although they do so in different ways!

FAST FACT

Warm-blooded sea animals, such as whales, have a thick, jelly-like layer of fatty **BLUBBER** under their skin. This works like a coat to keep in body heat. The bowhead whale has blubber more than 50 centimetres thick!

bowhead whale

WHAT'S THE TEMPERATURE?

Home bath: **39–40°C**
Warmest sea water: **35°C**
Tropical coral reef: **30°C**

Cold tap at home: **7–10°C**
Bottom of the deep sea: **2–3°C**
Coldest sea water: **–2°C**

icefish

Cold-blooded **FISH** are usually the same temperature as the water around them. Polar fish, such as icefish, have chemicals in their blood to stop them freezing solid.

Greenland sleeper

SLEEPER SHARKS are huge and old. The Greenland sleeper reaches more than 6 metres in length and lives for over 350 years! They are called "sleepers" because they stay still in the icy water for long periods.

rockhopper penguins

PENGUINS have layers of feathers to keep warm. They include long, strong feathers on the outside and two kinds of short, fluffy feathers underneath. A penguin is a cosy 38 degrees Celsius inside – a bit warmer than you!

MEET THE MAMMALS!

The main groups of sea mammals are cetaceans, such as dolphins and whales; pinnipeds, such as sea-lions, walruses and seals; and sirenians, such as dugongs and manatees.

The **DALL'S PORPOISE** looks like a mini killer whale. It prefers cool northern waters where it dives down 100 metres or more to feed on fish and squid.

Slim and fast, the 3-metre-long **LEOPARD SEAL** prowls the Southern Ocean around Antarctica. Its favourite food is penguins – although it spits out the feathers!

DUGONGS live around the coasts of the Indian and West Pacific Oceans. They are called "sea cows" because they spend hours feeding on seagrass plants.

As the second-biggest animal in the world, the **FIN WHALE** is slim, sleek and speedy. It reaches a speed of 50 kilometres per hour – faster than the quickest human runner!

The smallest sea mammal is not from one of the main groups; it's the **SEA OTTER** of North American coasts. It weighs just 30 kilograms.

Thousands of **COMMON DOLPHINS** gather in groups, called pods. These dolphins often leap in the air.

At more than 4 tonnes, the massive male **ELEPHANT SEAL** weighs as much as an elephant!

TOP 10 DEADLY ANIMALS

These animals can be dangerous to people – and some are truly deadly!

 Great white shark

The great white shark carries out some of the 50–100 shark attacks each year – but usually fewer than 10 people die.

2 Blue-ringed octopus

Beware this octopus if its rings glow blue! This means it may bite, and its bite can kill!

3 Barracuda

If a great barracuda comes near humans, it's usually just curious. But a sudden movement can cause it to bite with needle-sharp teeth.

4 Crown-of-thorns starfish

This big, spiny starfish has extremely powerful venom that causes pain, bleeding and swelling.

5 Stingray

Lying peacefully on the seabed, the stingray may strike if suddenly disturbed. Its dagger-like sting is on the underside of its tail.

6 Sea wasp (boxjelly)

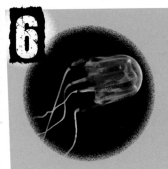

At 30 centimetres across, with long, trailing tentacles, the sea wasp can cause one of the world's most painful stings!

7 Stonefish

Lying on a weedy rock, the stonefish is so well camouflaged it is easy to step on. The spines on its back jab in a strong venom that can cause death.

8 Sea-snake

Sea-snakes spend all their life at sea. Their venom can kill a human, but they usually use it to kill fish.

9 Coneshell

This sea-snail may look slow and harmless. But a quick jab from its short, sharp, dart-like spine causes extreme pain – and can even be fatal.

10 Bull shark

Bull sharks are smaller than great whites, but more aggressive! Attacks blamed on great whites are often by bull sharks.

Which deadly animal is the most terrifying?

CLOSE UP

OCEAN WANDERER

About one metre long, loggerheads are medium-sized sea turtles. They live in the warm waters of the Atlantic and Pacific. Each year, they swim with currents to find their favourite foods. Some of them cross the entire Pacific Ocean, between the east coast of East Asia and the west coast of North America, and then back again.

More about loggerheads:

Length: 90 centimetres
Average lifespan: 50 years
Food: Crabs, conchs and jellyfish
Female loggerheads return to the beach
where they hatched to lay their own eggs.

KILLER WHALES

Your questions about killer whales answered – including why they are also called orcas!

Why do we call them "orcas"?

The nickname "orca" comes from an ancient Roman god of the underworld, Orcus. Orcas are also nicknamed "blackfish" because of their skin. Of course, orcas are not fish at all; they are mammals! Orcas are not whales either; they are really the biggest kind of dolphin!

killer whale hunting fish

What do killer whales kill?

Killer whales are so fast and powerful that they can kill almost anything they wish – to eat, of course! Some killers form big, settled groups, called pods, that stay near to shore and eat mainly fish. Others live in smaller pods that travel more widely and hunt mostly sea mammals, such as whales, dolphins, seals and sea lions.

Are killer whales clever?

Killer whales are among the most intelligent animals on the Earth! They can remember where and when prey is plentiful each year. They also work together to surround and catch shoals of fish, "talking" to each other using different noises, such as squeals and clicks.

Where do killer whales live?

Killer whales live in almost every sea and ocean around the world, with a total of about 50,000 living in the wild. They are most common in cool and cold waters and near to shore, and less common out in the middle of the open ocean and in warm, tropical regions.

SEA LIGHTS

Even on the brightest day, in the clearest sea, light soon fades with depth. Below 500 metres, there is no sunlight at all. Yet there are strange glimmers and flashes all around because many sea animals can make their own glowing light, known as **bioluminescence**! They glow and shine to communicate with each other, camouflage their body or lure prey.

FAST FACT

BIOFLUORESCENCE, as shown by this anemone, is a neon glow in some animals. These animals absorb light and then give it off again as a different colour. Biofluorescent animals are not able to turn their lights on and off like bioluminescent animals can.

anemone with clownfish

plankton

FAST FACT

Sometimes, parts of the ocean can appear to twinkle. This is due to types of bioluminescent **PLANKTON**. When the plankton sense movement, such as a wave or a boat, each one flashes – as a group, they twinkle!

FAST FACT

Sparkly **COMB JELLYFISH**, such as this sea walnut, are not bioluminescent. They have tiny cilia (moving hairs) that ripple along long bands that look like combs. The cilia reflect and scatter light, making the jelly sparkle!

sea walnut

dwarf lanternfish

FAST FACT

The bioluminescent **LANTERNFISH** has light-producing organs called photophores along its body. It glows to attract a mate and possibly to confuse predators by disguising its body shape.

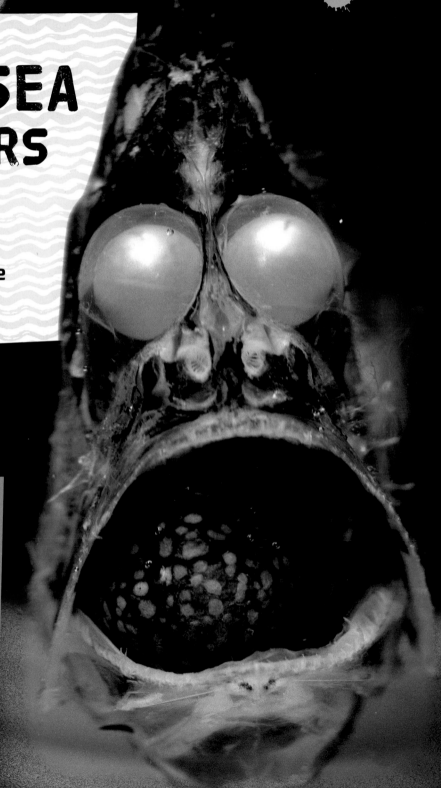

BOTTOM 10

DEEP-SEA DWELLERS

The strangest creatures live at the bottom of the deepest oceans.

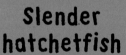

1 Slender hatchetfish

This fish has binocular vision, which means it can zoom in to view something far away – just like you can with a pair of binoculars!

2 Deep-sea anglerfish

Anglers have a head spine with a glowing tip to attract small fish and other prey – a bit like a fishing rod!

7 Hadal snailfish

This fish is found over 8000 metres deep! It may be called snailfish, but it has a tadpole-like tail.

3 Giant isopod

The giant isopod can grow to 70 centimetres long! It scavenges for bits of food sinking from above.

8 Fangtooth

This fish has two fangs that are so long its head needs sockets to fit them when its mouth is closed – a bit like a plug!

4 Gulper or pelican eel

This fish is almost all mouth! Its jaws open wide so it can swallow prey bigger than itself.

9 Dumbo octopus

This octopus has fin flaps that look like the ears of the cartoon elephant *Dumbo*. It lives up to 7000 metres deep!

5 Ratfish

A relative of sharks, this fish is also called rabbitfish or chimaera. It has a venomous fin spine on its back.

10 Bobtail squid

This squid has glowing bacteria in its mantle (body), to which it feeds a sugary fluid. The bacteria disguise it from predators!

6 Sea cucumber

The sea cucumber grows up to 1 metre long. It slides along the ocean floor, finding food in the mud and ooze.

Which deep-sea dweller is your number one?

OCEAN TREASURES

Seas and oceans provide many of our everyday needs – from important fuels to tasty fish fingers!

ISLAND PEOPLE catch fish, shellfish and other foods. They aim to take enough for themselves and to sell locally, and leave the rest for the future.

* Half of the Earth's **GAS** and **OIL** comes from under the sea. These fossil fuels are used to make plastics, paints, road surfaces and hundreds of other products.

* Large numbers of **WIND TURBINES** in the sea are called wind farms. They turn the energy of moving air into electricity. Electricity is also made by tidal and wave power stations.

* Precious **METALS**, **MINERALS** and **GEMS** come from mud and rocks under the sea. They include gold, silver and even diamonds! They are scooped up by mechanical grabs or sucked up by massive tubes.

* More than 90 per cent of the products you buy in shops are **TRANSPORTED** by sea. From toys to mobile phones, TVs to trucks – the list is endless!

* In some places, people use saltpans or artificial ponds full of seawater to farm the **SALT** you put in your food!

* **ARCHAEOLOGY** is the study of civilizations, buildings, art and other remains, such as shipwrecks! There could be over three million shipwrecks on the ocean floor. Archaeology in the ocean is called "marine archaeology".

CLOSE UP

BEACH LIFE

Surfers love big, crashing waves, or "breakers", which can reach more than 20 metres tall in places such as Hawaii, USA and Nazare, Portugal. When a wave makes a tunnel like this, surfers call it a "barrel" or "tube" – experienced surfers can surf inside a tube!

barrel

Surfing stats:

Highest wave surfed: 23.77 metres
Longest single surf: 3 hours 55 min 2 seconds (male)
Longest single surf: 2 hours 18 min 24 seconds (female)
Longest wave surfed by a dog: 107.2 metres

SAVE OUR SEAS!

The world's seas and oceans face many threats, and most are because of human activities. But we can all help by making small changes to our daily lives!

fishing trawler

GLOBAL WARMING

The Earth's climate is changing because of human actions. Pollution causes the planet to get warmer – we call this global warming. Corals get their colours and much of their food from plant-like algae living in them. As the water grows warmer, the algae die, the coral loses its food and looks "bleached".

bleached coral

POLLUTION

Rubbish, such as glass or plastic bottles, floats in almost every ocean and sea. This is very dangerous for marine animals. Many creatures get tangled and cut in fishing nets. Turtles eat plastic bags because they look like their jellyfish food, and soon die.

lionfish meets bag

oil pollution

OVERFISHING

Huge fishing boats scoop so many fish from the sea that there aren't enough fish to breed young for the future. The vast fishing nets can catch dolphins, seals, turtles and other air-breathers. The nets stop these animals from reaching the surface to breathe, so they drown.

trapped turtle

YOU CAN HELP!

You can answer the SOS! Here are some tips:

- When you're at the coast or in the sea, avoid damaging rocks, seaweeds, animals and corals.

- Do not collect sea animals or plants. Leave them as part of the natural habitat.

- Do not buy souvenirs of dead animals, such as starfish and seahorses.

- Recycle plastic, glass and other materials. This prevents them getting into the sea, and saves natural resources taken from the sea.

- Save clean water where you can. This means less water is taken from seas, rivers and lakes, and less energy is used to make it clean.

souvenir seahorse

TOP 10 WATER SPORTS!

There's always something to do by the ocean – or in it!

Flyboarding

Invented in 2012, the flyboard is connected to a hose that spurts water or air down, shooting the flyboard up at up to 150 kilometres per hour!

2 Windsurfing

The windsurfer uses wind power to move. It can reach an incredible 52 knots – 96 kilometres per hour!

3 Scuba diving

It is exciting to be part of the undersea world! "Scuba" means "**s**elf-**c**ontained **u**nderwater **b**reathing **a**pparatus".

4 Jet skis

Water jets out of the back, making the jet ski race forwards. Jet skis can do amazing stunts!

5 Kitesurfing

More than two million kitesurfers belong to clubs worldwide. Experts can do more than 10 somersaults in mid-air!

6 Sailing

There are so many kinds of sailing craft, from small dinghies to huge, sleek ocean yachts. Sailing is an Olympic sport!

7 Paragliding

Beginner paragliders are towed by a boat, but experts steer wherever they wish – even landing on a moving boat!

8 Powerboats

The fastest powerboats roar along at more than 250 kilometres per hour, which is twice the motorway speed limit!

9 Surfing

Island people have been surfing for centuries! It became popular in the 1900s, when the modern board was invented.

10 Wakeboarders

Wakeboarders make amazing twists, turns, jumps and loops while zipping along at more than 40 kilometres per hour, towed behind a speedboat!

Which water sport is your number one?

THE OCEANS & SEAS QUIZ

Are you an expert on all things underwater? Test your knowledge by completing this quiz! When you've answered all of the questions, turn to page 63 to find your score.

 Which ocean is the smallest, shallowest and coldest?
a) Arctic Ocean
b) Atlantic Ocean
c) Indian Ocean

 Which ocean current does the blue shark use to travel to reach Europe?
a) The Gelf Stream
b) The Golf Stream
c) The Gulf Stream

 The Mid-Atlantic Ridge is an ...
a) Underwater mountain range
b) Underwater wall
c) Underwater volcano

 What is the Mariana Trench?
a) The coldest place on the Earth
b) The deepest place on the Earth
c) The highest place on the Earth

 How many seas are there on the Earth?
a) Less than 50
b) Less than 90
c) More than 100

 Mangroves grow on shores where ...
a) Currents are gentle
b) Currents are moderate
c) Currents are strong

 When an animal's colours and shape blend in with its surroundings, we call it ...
a) Camouflaged
b) Cornered
c) Covered up

 What percentage of the Earth's ocean animals live in coral reefs?
a) 10 %
b) 15 %
c) 25 %

 Which bird has the longest wings of all?
a) Albatross
b) Pelican
c) Puffin

 Which ocean creature is the biggest animal on the Earth?
a) Blue whale
b) Great white shark
c) Whale shark

 What is blubber?
a) A jelly-like layer of fat
b) A smooth layer of scales
c) A thick layer of fur

 How long can Greenland sleeper sharks live for?
a) Less than 50 years
b) About 150 years
c) More than 350 years

 How warm is a penguin under its feathers?
a) 25 degrees Celsius
b) 32 degrees Celsius
c) 38 degrees Celsius

 What is the name for a group of dolphins?
a) A pad
b) A pod
c) A putt

 How many shark attacks are there each year?
a) 10–50
b) 50–100
c) 100–1000

 Where do female loggerhead turtles lay their eggs?
a) In the coral reef
b) Near rocky cliffs
c) On the beach where they hatched

 Which animal is sometimes called an orca or blackfish?
a) Common dolphin
b) Killer whale
c) Sperm whale

 What was the longest wave surfed by a dog?
a) 10 metres
b) 55 metres
c) 107.2 metres

 Which of these sports is an Olympic sport?
a) Flyboarding
b) Sailing
c) Scuba diving

 Which ocean covers almost one-third of the Earth's surface?
a) The Atlantic Ocean
b) The Indian Ocean
c) The Pacific Ocean

GLOSSARY

atmosphere
The layer of gases that surround some planets and moons, including Earth.

bar
A long, low, narrow mound, usually made of sand, that may be underwater at high tide. Generally both ends are attached to the land.

bioluminescence
Light produced by living things. Many ocean animals are bioluminescent, as are glow-worms and fireflies on land.

blubber
A thick layer of fat under the skin of many polar and ocean creatures, which helps to keep them warm.

breeding
When a male and a female animal come together to produce young.

camouflage
The colours and patterns of an animal that help it to blend in with its surroundings. This disguise helps it to hide from predators or creep up on prey without being seen.

earthquake
A violent shaking felt on the Earth's surface, caused by sudden movements of its continents.

fissure
A narrow, deep, steep-sided crack or crevasse.

gravity
The force that attracts objects towards each other. The greater an object's mass, the greater its pull of gravity. Earth's tides are caused mainly by the Moon's gravity, and also the Sun's.

skeleton
The strong supporting framework of a living thing. Fish, amphibians, reptiles, birds and mammals have an inner skeleton of bones.

spit
A long, low narrow mound, usually of sand or shingle, that sticks out into the water, generally with one end attached to the land.

tornado
A tall, moving, funnel-shaped area of fast-spinning winds, usually beneath large storm clouds.

tropics
The areas of the Earth around the middle, about 2600 kilometres on either side of the Equator. They are usually warm all year around.

hurricane
A huge storm, hundreds of kilometres across, with swirling winds faster than 120 kilometres per hour, and massive amounts of rain.

lava
Hot, molten rock that erupts onto the surface of a planet and starts to flow.

low tide mark
The farthest point down the shore that the sea reaches at low tide. Below this mark is underwater all the time.

mountain range
A long row or chain of high peaks, on land or underwater.

seamount
A mountain that rises from the seabed, but its top or peak is underwater, not above the surface

shallow
Not deep, or not very far between the surface and bottom of the water.

shingle
Loose pebble and cobble stones, mostly up to about 20 centimetres across, usually rounded by being rubbed together.

QUIZ ANSWERS: 1 = a, 2 = c, 3 = a, 4 = b, 5 = c, 6 = a, 7 = a, 8 = c, 9 = a, 10 = a, 11 = a, 12 = c, 13 = c, 14 = b, 15 = b, 16 = c, 17 = b, 18 = c, 19 = b, 20 = c.

INDEX